EXPLORE
my world

Rain Forests

Marfé Ferguson Delano

NATIONAL
GEOGRAPHIC
KiDS

WASHINGTON, D.C.

Gleaming green leaves...

Deep, dark shade.
Hot, steamy air.
Soft ground beneath
your feet. Welcome
to the rain forest.

From lemon-colored snakes to lime-colored lizards ...

... from electric blue butterflies to petal pink bugs, rain forests are full of amazing animals.

Slither!

On the dark and shady forest floor, huge pythons slip through fallen twigs and leaves.

Enormous tarantulas tiptoe across roots. Poison dart frogs hop like jumping jewels.

9

Sleek tigers slink through shadows.

The forest floor is the bottom level of the rain forest.

Shaggy bears
shuffle along,
looking for fruit
and bugs to eat.

Swoosh!

Big bats swoop through leafy shrubs and twisting vines.

Billions of bugs creep, crawl, flit, and flutter.

In the understory, tree kangaroos climb, leopards lounge, and lizards leap.

The understory is the level of shrubs, vines, and small trees above the forest floor.

Roar!

High up in the canopy, howler monkeys whoop and roar. Macaws screech and toucans croak.

The canopy level is above the understory. It contains the leaves and branches of giant trees.

Here, hummingbirds zip from flower to flower, sparkling in the sunshine. Acrobatic monkeys swing from vine to vine.

Red-eyed tree frogs leap from branch to branch. Mossy-furred sloths hang still as statues.

Split, splat, splatter, boom!

A thunderstorm moves in. Rain pours onto the canopy and beats against the leaves.

It fills the cup-shaped plants called bromeliads with water that creatures will drink and live in.

It rolls down the tree trunks and drips off the vines onto the dark and shady forest floor.

Can you say bro-MEE-lee-ad?

Rain falls nearly every day. All the plants and animals in the rain forest, from orchids to owls to orangutans, depend upon the rain.

Drip, drop!

Rain is what makes the rain forest so rich and full of life. And it makes beautiful rainbows!

sloth

Rain Forest Layer Cake

A rain forest is like a cake with four layers stacked one atop the other. Each layer, or level, is a different neighbor-hood, with different kinds of animals living in it. Which layer would you most like to explore?

toucan

EMERGENT LAYER

The fourth layer is the emergent layer. It consists of the very tallest treetops, which poke above the canopy here and there.

CANOPY

The third layer is the canopy. It contains the leaves and branches of the towering trees that stretch over the rain forest like great green umbrellas. Flowers, ferns, and mosses grow on the bark of canopy trees. It is bright and sunny up here.

UNDERSTORY

The second layer is the understory. It is filled with shrubs, small trees, and thick vines winding their way toward the treetops.

FOREST FLOOR

The bottom layer is the forest floor. It is covered with roots, fallen leaves, and low-growing plants. It is very dark and shady here because the trees above it block most of the sunlight.

Rain Forests Around the World

Tropical rain forests are very special places. In fact, more than half of all the different plants and animals on Earth live in rain forests! That's why it is so important to protect rain forests and keep them healthy. The plants and animals that live there need their rain forest homes to survive.

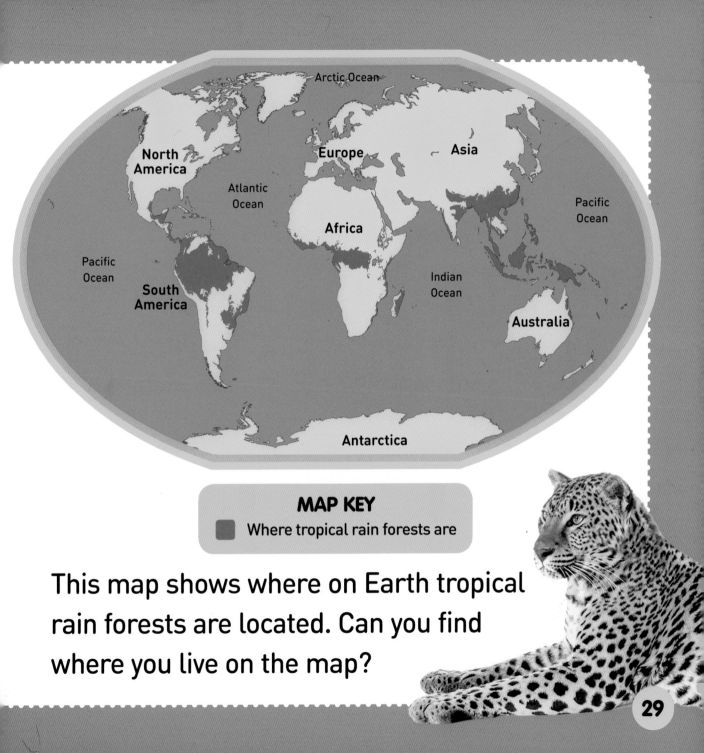

Arctic Ocean

North America

Europe

Asia

Atlantic Ocean

Pacific Ocean

Africa

Pacific Ocean

South America

Indian Ocean

Australia

Antarctica

MAP KEY

Where tropical rain forests are

This map shows where on Earth tropical rain forests are located. Can you find where you live on the map?

Hide-and-Seek

Some rain forest creatures are very good at hiding in plain sight. Can you spot the animal in each picture?

1. Asian horned frog 2. orchid mantis 3. gecko 4. thorn bugs 5. jaguar 6. stick insects

Name That Food

Many of the foods we love to eat today were first discovered growing in rain forests. Can you name the foods in these pictures? Which ones do you like most?

mangoes

orange

coffee beans

coconut

bananas

lemons

pineapple

chocolate

To Carolyn Holloway, wonderful aunt, sister, mother, teacher, and friend, with love—MFD

Since 1888, the National Geographic Society has funded more than 12,000 research, exploration, and preservation projects around the world. The Society receives funds from National Geographic Partners, LLC, funded in part by your purchase. A portion of the proceeds from this book supports this vital work. To learn more, visit natgeo.com/info.

NATIONAL GEOGRAPHIC and Yellow Border Design are trademarks of the National Geographic Society, used under license.

Library of Congress Cataloging-in-Publication Data

Names: National Geographic Society (U.S.)
Title: Explore my world rain forests.
Description: Washington, DC : National Geographic, [2017] | Series: Explore my world | Audience: Age 3-7. | Audience: Grade K to grade 3.
Identifiers: LCCN 2016050206 (print) | LCCN 2016059890 (ebook) | ISBN 9781426328282 (pbk. : alk. paper) | ISBN 9781426328299 (hardcover : alk. paper) | ISBN 9781426328305 (e-book)
Subjects: LCSH: Rain forests--Juvenile literature.
Classification: LCC QH86 .E97 2017 (print) | LCC QH86 (ebook) | DDC 577.34--dc23
LC record available at https://lccn.loc.gov/2016050206

Art director and designer: Sanjida Rashid
Project manager and editor: Ariane Szu-Tu
Photo editor: Christina Ascani

Printed in Hong Kong
17/THK/1

ILLUSTRATIONS CREDITS
Front cover: Michael Gore/Minden Pictures; Back cover: Martin Harvey/Getty Images; 1 (CTR), Jeff Foott/Minden Pictures; 2–3 (CTR), Anup Shah/Minden Pictures; 4–5 (CTR), simonlong/Getty Images; 6 (UP LE), Thomas Marent/Minden Pictures; 6 (UP), Milous Chab/Dreamstime; 6 (LO), Ben Sadd/Minden Pictures; 7 (CTR), Chien Lee/Minden Pictures; 8 (LE), Stu Porter/Alamy Stock Photo; 9 (UP), CraigBurrows/Shutterstock; 9 (LO), Danita Delimont/Getty Images; 10 (UP), Theo Allofs/Minden Pictures; 10 (LO), Tim Laman/Getty Images; 11 (CTR), Rajiv Welikala/Alamy Stock Photo; 12 (CTR), Patrick Kientz/Minden Pictures; 13 (UP), Paul van Hoof/Minden Pictures; 13 (CTR), Nick Garbutt/Minden Pictures; 13 (RT), Hiroya Minakuchi/Minden Pictures; 14 (UP LE), Gerry Ellis/Minden Pictures; 14 (UP RT), Richard Du Toit/Minden Pictures; 14–15 (RT), Stephen Dalton/Minden Pictures; 16, Mark Bowler/Minden Pictures; 17 (UP), Luciano Candisani/Minden Pictures; 17 (LO), Konrad Wothe/Minden Pictures; 18 (UP), Jami Tarris/Getty Images; 18 (LO LE), Kevin Elsby/Minden Pictures; 18 (LO RT), Tim Fitzharris/Minden Pictures; 19 (CTR), David Tipling/Getty Images; 20 (LE), DG-Photography/Getty Images; 21 (UP RT), Clay_Harrison/Getty Images; 21 (LO LE), Luciano Candisani/Minden Pictures; 21 (LO RT), ZSSD/Minden Pictures; 22 (UP), johnandersonphoto/Getty Images; 22 (LO), Neil Bowman/Minden Pictures; 23 (CTR), Thomas Marent/Minden Pictures; 24–25 (CTR), Niebrugge Images/Alamy Stock Photo; 26 (UP LE), Panoramic Images/Getty Images; 26 (CTR), jeremyreds/Getty Images; 27 (UP), Hiroya Minakuchi/Getty Images; 27 (UP CTR), SimonLong/Getty Images; 27 (LO CTR), Richard Price/Getty Images; 27 (LO), Jason Edwards/Getty Images; 28 (UP RT), Dobermaraner/Shutterstock; 28 (LO LE), Tim Davis/Corbis/VCG/Getty Images; 29 (LO), Lenor Ko/Shutterstock; 30 (UP LE), Thomas Marent/Minden Pictures; 30 (UP CTR), Alex Hyde/Minden Pictures; 30 (UP RT), Thomas Marent/Minden Pictures; 30 (LO LE), Stephen Dalton/Minden Pictures; 30 (LO CTR), Aditya Singh/Getty Images; 30 (LO RT), Konrad Wothe/Minden Pictures; 31 (UP), Maks Narodenko/Shutterstock; 31 (LE), Maks Narodenko/Shutterstock; 31 (CTR), NinaM/Shutterstock; 31 (CTR), Christian Jung/Shutterstock; 31 (CTR), Viktar Malyshchyts/Shutterstock; 31 (RT), Evgeny Karandaev/Shutterstock; 31 (LO), Lukas Gojda/Shutterstock; 31 (LO RT), Photodisc; 32 (UP), Suzi Esztergas/Minden Pictures